THE ATTITUDE OF THE ANCIENT EGYPTIANS TO DEATH & THE DEAD

T0346181

THE ATTITUDE OF THE ANCIENT EGYPTIANS TO DEATH & THE DEAD

by

ALAN H. GARDINER

D.Litt., F.B.A.

THE FRAZER LECTURE
FOR 1935 : DELIVERED IN THE
UNIVERSITY OF CAMBRIDGE
ON THE 14TH OF MAY
1935

CAMBRIDGE
AT THE UNIVERSITY PRESS
1935

CAMBRIDGE
UNIVERSITY PRESS

University Printing House, Cambridge CB2 8BS, United Kingdom

Published in the United States of America by Cambridge University Press, New York

Cambridge University Press is part of the University of Cambridge.

It furthers the University's mission by disseminating knowledge in the pursuit of education, learning and research at the highest international levels of excellence.

www.cambridge.org
Information on this title: www.cambridge.org/9781107689268

© Cambridge University Press 1935

This publication is in copyright. Subject to statutory exception and to the provisions of relevant collective licensing agreements, no reproduction of any part may take place without the written permission of Cambridge University Press.

First published 1935
Re-issued 2014

A catalogue record for this publication is available from the British Library

ISBN 978-1-107-68926-8 Paperback

Cambridge University Press has no responsibility for the persistence or accuracy of URLs for external or third-party internet websites referred to in this publication, and does not guarantee that any content on such websites is, or will remain, accurate or appropriate.

THE ATTITUDE OF
THE ANCIENT EGYPTIANS TO
DEATH AND THE DEAD

To explain the intense preoccupation of the
Ancient Egyptians with death and the hereafter
requires a complex and exceptional set of con-
ditions. Some[1] have pointed to the unique climate
of Egypt, where one cloudless day succeeds
another, and where the air is so dry that, as Sir
Flinders Petrie has put it, the problem is rather to
discover why anything should perish than why it
should survive. Where permanence is thus the
rule, could man be the exception? But this explanation is obviously insufficient to account for
more than a general bias on the side of survival,
nor indeed can we hope to divine all the reasons
for the extraordinary funerary activity which we
associate with mummification and the Pyramids.
One contributory factor is found in the obser-
vation that the selfsame preservative quality of the
climate which has filled our museums with papyri
and has maintained intact the most delicate of

(5)

woven tissues tends also to give unusual prominence to the fact of death. Go up into the high desert fringing the Nile Valley, and you will hardly fail to descry the skull or thigh-bone of some quadruped. The earliest inhabitants, seeking new burial-places for their relatives, must constantly have been coming upon well-preserved human skeletons, bringing home to their minds more emphatically than elsewhere the disturbing but indisputable reality of death.[2] The shock of such discoveries may have gone far towards inducing the frame of mind we are seeking to explain. In no country of the earth is life more attractive, more desirable; yet in no other country is death so nakedly revealed. Little wonder that the Egyptians conceived a fanatical abhorrence of death, and devoted no small part of their wealth to devising means of defeating it. This fundamental trait in their psychology is well brought out in the initial words of the appeal which, on many a Middle Kingdom sepulchral stela, exhorts passers-by to utter a prayer on behalf of the deceased: *O ye who live and exist, who love life and hate death....*[3]

The subject upon which I am addressing you this afternoon was suggested by a reply once given by me to the great scholar whose name is connected with this lecture. Sir James Frazer has produced testimony from all quarters of the globe[4] to show how prevalent is the fear of the dead, and how great an influence that fear has exerted upon early customs and behaviour. To his question whether the same fear was much in evidence in Ancient Egypt I replied with an unequivocal negative, and I must confess that this assertion of mine, over-categorically made, has weighed somewhat heavily on my conscience. To be invited to deliver the Frazer lecture in Cambridge was an honour I could not have resisted in any case; but for me it possessed the additional attraction of giving an opportunity to examine this matter afresh, and my present purpose is to define my position more closely, and to state my conclusions with whatever reserves may seem necessary.

At the outset it must be realized that to fear death and to fear the dead are two very different things, though of course they are by no means incompatible, and when combined may very well lead to ancestor-worship, as has happened in China. But of a cult of the ancestors in the Chinese sense there is very little trace in Egypt.[5] Filial obedience was indeed enjoined, and that a son should piously attend to the funerary needs of his parents was the thought underlying the entire ritual of the temples, where the Pharaoh, in practice represented by an officiant priest, typified Horus in the act of supplying the material needs of his father Osiris.[6] The same thought underlay, in theory at least, the relations of the living and the dead. The reigning king will undoubtedly, in the best of cases, have taken some active part in celebrating the cult of the dead man who was at once his father and his predecessor, and this example will have been followed by the nobles in respect of their dead, and also by the common people. There can be no doubt, of course, that a son could usually be counted upon to give his parents decent burial, or failing a son some other close relative.[7] A false-door or other adjuncts might also be added to the tomb after the owner's death.[8] We may also conjecture that filial piety as

a rule prompted the presentation of daily offerings at least during the first few months of bereave-
ment.[9] But we have highly significant evidence,
of which I shall say more later, that for the per-
petuation of such offerings the Egyptian nobles of
the Old and Middle Kingdoms preferred to rely
upon definite contractual arrangements.[10] In the
absence of such, funerary observances can seldom
have extended to the grandparents, let alone re-
moter ancestry. Only in the practice of Pharaoh
himself was there any serious exception to this rule.
Occasionally a king dedicated a statue or made
offerings to some distinguished predecessor, and
in the temple of Abydos Sethos I is represented as
offering to all the legitimate kings of Egypt from
Menes downwards. Thus the degree to which
ancestors were commemorated and tended in
Egypt is extremely limited, so much so that as
a generalization it is permissible to affirm that
ancestor-worship was not among the habits of the
Ancient Egyptians.

After these prefatory remarks I will now con-
centrate upon the question as to how far the
Egyptians feared their dead, and in order to give

my answer its proper background I will attempt
to characterize their general outlook on life from
a very wide perspective. The logicality of the
Egyptian mind is one of its most striking aspects,
and nothing is more remarkable than the impar-
tiality with which the living, the dead and the
gods were regarded. *Men, gods, dead*[11]—this and
similar collocations of words are not infrequently
found, and indicate a hierarchical classification of
human and superhuman beings which is reflected
in many other conceptions and in much of the
behaviour of this ancient people. All three classes
had the same needs and were treated in the same
manner. The temple was called ⌐🔲⌐ *ḥet-nātjer*
"the god's castle", just as a living prince possessed
his 🔲〰️♀♀♀🔲 *per en ʿankhyw* "house of the
living",[12] and just as also the tomb was often
described as a man's 🔲⌐〰️🔲 *ḥet ent enḥeḥ* "castle
of eternity"[13]—ἀιδίους οἴκους is the term used
by Diodorus.[14] In actual fact temple, tomb, and
house of the living all bore a strong resemblance
to one another, containing rooms where the
owner lived, and others where his possessions
were stored. A significant detail is that some

tombs of the Second Dynasty were found to contain unmistakable privies.[15] Just as a wealthy landowner possessed his 𓀀𓀀𓀀 "servants" (*ḥemu*), so too the gods and the dead possessed theirs; the name for the highest class of priests was 𓊹𓊹𓊹𓊹 *ḥemu-nātjer* "servants of the god", and the dead were ministered to by 𓊹𓀀 *ḥemu-ka* "*ka*-servants" or "soul-servants". Funerary and divine rites conformed to the model provided by human needs; just as living men required food and clothing, so too did the dead and the gods; the only differences were that the latter, in order to obtain their requirements, had to be brought to life again by magical passes (the so-called 𓌹𓏤 *wep-ro* "opening-of-the-mouth" ceremony) and that the presentation of garments and food-offerings had to be accompanied by appropriate gestures and by the recitation of prescribed words, these usually reminiscent of the story of Osiris. Exactly like human beings the gods were deemed to have lived on earth, to have had their sorrows and their joys, to have married wives and to have begotten children, and at last to have died. Even the number of years they lived

(11)

was recorded.[16] The conception of the sun-god being born every morning, growing old during the course of the day, and dying at sunset is not particularly relevant in this connexion, since here we have poetical imagery rather than accepted belief. But the story of the murdered and resurrected god Osiris is very much to the point. This most important of all Egyptian deities was definitely conceived of as an ancient king who, when he died, had been succeeded by his son Horus, and if he continued to live at all, it was partly as ruler of the netherworld and partly as the local divinity of Busiris and Abydos. In the latter aspect Osiris ran the risk of perishing afresh, for magicians sometimes threatened that, unless their will prevailed, they would *cast fire into Busiris and burn up Osiris*.[17]

These strange notions of the gods as once having died but as still, in a different sense, living and exerting power are found also in connexion with mankind. That men die in the ordinary physical way was as clear to the Egyptians as it is to all the world, and in some instances they even held that death might be total annihilation. When the

Pharaoh slays his enemies, the inscriptions state that he destroys them *as though they had never been*,[18] and as regards their own destiny the Egyptians evidently feared that they too might perish utterly and irretrievably. This indeed was the underlying presupposition of all their funereal preparations. But if all the precautions taken should prove successful, then physical death might be a mere transition[19] from one state of life to another—the second life being not indeed quite the same as had been lived *upon earth*, not quite the same as when a man was *standing upon his feet*, but as close a replica as the imagination would allow. Thus the names of dead persons in inscriptions of the Eighteenth Dynasty are frequently followed by the epithet *wahem ꜥānekh* "living again", more literally "repeating life". The life after corporeal death was, however, liable to all the vicissitudes of the first. Hunger and thirst might assail it, and a special dread of the Egyptians, often mentioned in the Coffin Texts and the Book of the Dead, was that in the future life they might be reduced to eating their own excrements.[20] Many similar fears are voiced in the headings of spells contained in the two collections of funerary texts just referred to. Thus there were spells for preventing a man *from decaying in the necropolis*,[21] *from having his head cut off in the necropolis*,[22] *from being accused by his heart in the necropolis*,[23] and most significant of all, *from dying a second death*.[24] The obvious implication of this last expression is that the second death would be final and absolute.

The trend of my argument has been to show that in Egyptian belief men, gods and dead were beings all very much on a same level, subject to like joys and sorrows, sharing the same risks, requiring similar nourishment and apparel, and ultimately liable, unless forethought and magic could stave it off, to a real and irreparable death. In a world of beings thus homogeneously constituted there was little room for fear, except in so far as one man feared another. It is to this last proviso that I now turn, since it helps to give the answer to Sir James Frazer's question. In terrestrial life those men inspire fear who are obviously dangerous and harmful. Now in the realms of the gods and the dead there would naturally be the same moral differences as among the living. Just as there were good men and bad men, so too there were good gods and bad gods, good dead and bad dead. The bad would naturally inspire fear, but the good would not. It is true that in this respect the three classes of beings were not all quite on the same footing. Many of the gods, for example Shu, Tefēnet, Gēb or Sobk, were too far removed from human interests to have been labelled with any particular moral valuation. The great gods Rēꜥ and Osiris, on the other hand, were universally regarded as beneficent and just, whilst Bast and Sakhmet, on the contrary, were dreaded as being dangerous and vengeful goddesses. The position of Seth, the murderer of Osiris, was rather anomalous, and reflects various stages in his complex evolution. Through his rôle in the Osirian drama the thought of him was naturally always associated with violence and turbulence, and there were moments in Egyptian history when his name was deliberately expunged from the monuments. In contradiction to this view was his cult in particular cities like Ombos and Oxyrhynchos, and under the kings of the Nineteenth Dynasty Seth actually became one of the principal gods of the realm, as he had previously been under the Hyksos.

As regards the dead, different degrees of moral estimation prevailed just as among the gods and among the living. Indeed the only difference between the living and the dead in this respect was that the latter, in so far as they still haunted their early habitations, were on account of their invisibility the more readily suspected of evil intentions. The living you can see and guard yourself against, however ill-disposed. On the contrary the dead spirit who, as one text describes him, *comes in darkness and enters slinking in*,[25] was far more likely to be on some errand of mischief, and to that extent was more truly to be feared. However, neither fear nor yet reverence, its worthier counterpart, seems to have been much developed in the Egyptian psychological make-up. The ancient records display the Egyptians as an exceptionally light-hearted and individualistic race, singularly little troubled with regard for their fellows, whether living, dead or divine.[26] I have already alluded in passing to the threats habitually levelled by magicians against such deities as refused to do their bidding. The trait is so contrary to the feeling of other peoples of the earth that Iamblichus explicitly named the Egyptians as unique on this account.[27] The very prevalent crime of tomb-robbery is strong testimony to the absence of any overwhelming fear of the dead, and the curses which nobles of the Old Kingdom called upon the heads of would-be desecrators of the mastabas tell their own story.[28] The pyramid of Amenemmes I at Lisht is largely constructed out of the fragments of earlier sepulchres. Among the Middle Kingdom coffins studied by Dr. de Buck and myself not a few had been used twice over. From the Twentieth Dynasty we have a whole series of papyri, now preserved in London, Liverpool and elsewhere, recounting the depredations and confessions of systematic plunderers of the royal tombs at Thebes.[29] Even more cogent is the unwritten evidence. Excavators hardly ever light upon an untouched tomb.[30] When such occurs, as may with some qualification be said about the tomb of Tutʿankhamūn, unusual inaccessibility or other exceptional circumstances can as a rule be assigned as the reason.

On the other side of the account must be placed the spells directed against the dead which are a regular feature of the magical and magico-medical papyri. These do betray at least a certain degree of fear of the dead. To explain the facts of illness and of death the Egyptians felt themselves driven, in the last resort, to assume malign influence on the part of the dead. There is nothing commoner in this abundant class of texts than formulae banning *every dead man or dead woman, every enemy male or female, who shall work evil against N., the son of M.*[31] We must suppose that the mischievous dead here in question were mainly such as had never received decent burial or whose tombs had subsequently been destroyed. Mainly such, I say, but not entirely, since we find cases where magicians threaten damage to the tombs of dead men who should prove themselves ill-disposed.[32] It would be easy, however, to overestimate the importance of the formulae directed against mischief-working dead persons. In the first place they alternate with sober prescriptions almost modern in their enumeration of drugs and in their directions as to the manner of use. In the second place, recourse to the theory of interference on the part of the dead was only one of the ways in which death and malady were explained. In the texts we often find death accounted for as due to scorpion-sting, snake-bite, falling from a wall, drowning, or the blow inflicted by some enemy.[33] A hitherto unknown aetiology of death appears to be mentioned in an unpublished papyrus of the Twentieth Dynasty belonging to the French Archaeological Institute in Cairo. This describes the varying symptoms which enabled one to tell whether a dying man was under the influence of Rēʿ or of Osiris or of some other of the great gods. The conception seems to be novel, and I mention it here only for that reason.

Hitherto we have been concerned solely with the relations of the living with the unknown dead, and I now turn to the relations of the Egyptians with the dead of their own families. Passages can be cited from all periods to show that protection and succour were expected from deceased parents,[34] who for that reason will have been regarded with love and confidence, the very reverse of fear. On the other hand Egyptologists have long known a pathetic letter addressed by a widower to his dead wife, whom he claims to have treated with every kindness and who now, at least so he believes, is inflicting all manner of evil upon him. The document is so full of human touches, that I will take leave to read you a free translation:[35]

To the excellent Spirit ʿAnkhere! What wicked thing have I done to thee that I should have come to this evil pass? What have I done to thee? But what *thou* hast done is to have laid hands on me, although I had done nothing wicked to thee. From the time I lived with thee as thy husband down to today, what have I done to thee that I need hide? But what *thou* hast done is that I should have to bring this accusation against thee. I will lay a plaint against thee with words of my mouth in the presence of the Nine gods who are in the West, and it shall be decided between thee and this letter. What have I done to thee? I made thee a married woman in my youth. I lived with thee whilst acting in all kinds of posts. I lived with thee, and did not put thee away. I did not allow thee to grieve. This I did whilst I was a youth, and whilst I was filling all manner of important posts for Pharaoh, without putting thee away, for

I said: She has always been with me. And everyone who came to me when I was in thy presence, for thy sake I did not receive them, thinking that I would fall in with thy wishes. And now, behold, thou dost not suffer my heart to find comfort. Therefore I will be judged with thee, so that one shall discern right from wrong. Behold, while I was training officers for Pharaoh's infantry and cavalry, I caused them to come and lie prostrate on their bellies before thee, bringing all manner of good things to lay before thee, and I concealed nothing from thee as long as thou livedst. I did not give thee pain through anything that I did, acting as a lord. Nor didst thou find me flouting thee by behaving like a peasant and entering into a strange house. I caused no man to find fault with me in anything that I did with thee. And when they placed me in the position in which I am, I became unable to go abroad in my wonted fashion, so I did the thing that a man in my position usually does as regards thy ointment, thy provisions and thy clothes, and I did not dispose of them elsewhere on the pretext that "the woman is away". But behold, thou dost not recognize the good which I have done to thee, so I write to let thee know what *thou* art doing. When thou didst sicken of the illness which thou hadst, I caused a master-physician to be fetched, and he gave thee treatment, and did everything which thou didst command. And when I accompanied Pharaoh to the South and this condition had befallen thee, I spent eight months without eating and drinking like a man. And when I arrived in Memphis, I sought leave of Pharaoh, and came to the place where thou wast, and wept exceedingly together with my household in front of my street-quarter. And I gave linen clothes to wrap thee, and caused many clothes to be made, and left no benefit undone that had to be performed for thee. And now behold, I have spent three years (alone) without entering into a house, though it is not right that one like me should have to do it. This I have done for thy sake. But behold, thou dost not know good from bad. Therefore judgement shall be made between thee and me.

Until comparatively recently this letter, which dates from the Twentieth Dynasty or thereabouts, was believed to be unique, but in 1928 the late Professor Sethe collaborated with me in editing seven further letters to the dead of much earlier date,[36] and since the appearance of our book a couple more have been added.[37] Most of these remarkable documents are written in hieratic on the inside or outside of earthenware dishes or bowls, and nearly all range from the Sixth to the Twelfth Dynasty. They are invariably addressed to some close member of the family, to a dead husband, mother or father whose assistance is sought. Some meagre food-offerings may or may not have been placed in the vessel, and this was undoubtedly deposited upon the tomb of the addressee. Usually the writer starts with a reminder of old times, for example recalling some service rendered by himself, or else some promise given by the dead relative. Next follows the petition or grievance. In one case a woman and her son are being robbed of their property, in another case a maid-servant, the mainstay of the home, is seriously ill, and in a third case a male child is asked for. A constant feature consists of hints concerning the sinister influence exerted by some other dead person or persons, against whom the addressee is begged to intervene, sometimes even by taking legal proceedings. The language employed is always allusive and obscure, and not infrequently interpretation becomes impossible. But one thing is clear about these letters to the dead. They disclose a view of things according to which family affections and antipathies retained their strength almost untrammelled by the fact of death. The prayer urging a dead mother to arbitrate between the writer and a hostile dead brother is typical. It is as though death had no more effect than to set a barrier analogous to that of physical distance. Except in so far as such a barrier existed, all went on just as before. Some relatives were friendly, others were unfriendly. Only the latter were feared when dead, and if they were feared, it was not because they were dead but for other reasons.

If thus the living Egyptians were not particularly afraid of their dead, the latter had all the more reason to be afraid of the living. Here we touch upon the mainspring of all Egyptian funerary observances.[38] The Egyptians were literally panic-stricken as to what might be done or might happen to them after their deaths. With their amazingly logical and material and self-centred outlook, they imagined that all their earthly needs would persist, though at the same time they were acutely aware that somehow they would no longer be able to look after them. Hence all manner of precautions had to be taken and costly preparations made while they were still alive. Their bodies had to be kept from falling to pieces, and from this consideration arose the practice of mummification.[39] But since their mummies were decked out with precious jewels, and since their weapons and utensils lay all around them, a terror now obsessed them lest they should be robbed by the living. For that reason mummy and burial equipment were hidden away as inaccessibly as possible, at the bottom of deep tomb-shafts, often a hundred feet or more below the earth. Even so a dead man was not safe, and consequently the walls of his burial-chamber or the sides of his sarcophagus had to be covered with written spells designed for his protection and welfare. But the very hieroglyphs used for this purpose were not without their dangers. These hieroglyphs included miniature figures of men, animals and reptiles, to render which powerless it became a practice early in the Old Kingdom to deprive them of their legs or bodies, to chop them in half, or even to replace them with safer substitutes.[40]

The custom of making the actual burial-chamber as remote as possible had one serious inconvenience: it was no longer practicable to place a dead man's food immediately in front of him. From the Fourth Dynasty onwards the usual tomb of a nobleman was a solid stone-lined structure of great size built above and around the burial-shaft. Such a tomb is known to Egyptologists as a maṣṭaba, from an Arabic word meaning a bench. A small chamber with a false door in its rear was constructed in or against the east wall of the maṣṭaba,[41] and behind this, invisible except through a chink in the stone, was enclosed a life-size statue of the dead man, a substitute for himself which after being magically imbued with life could accept the offerings brought to him.[42] But who was to bring these offerings? As already pointed out, a man could not trust his kith and kin to perform this essential service out of mere piety. Hence it became necessary for nobles to make contracts for food-offerings during their own life-times. A considerable amount of property in land was usually set aside for the purpose, and a number of *ka*-priests, as they were called, were given endowments from this property on condition that they should regularly provide the dead man with food. Such *ka*-priests might or might not be the children of the deceased, but the essential point is that their willingness to serve was secured by contracts made by a man on his own behalf whilst he was still alive.[43] Needless to say, in the lack of legal enforcement such contracts lapsed all too easily not long after their author's demise. When this happened, and after the tomb had been wrecked and plundered, all that was left to its owner was the despairing hope that his name might be remembered[44] or that a funerary formula might be pronounced on his behalf by some kindly passer-by.[45] To what straits the dead might be reduced is indicated by the words sometimes accompanying the request for such a funerary prayer: *The breath of the mouth is useful to the noble dead. This is not a thing of which one should grow weary, for it is more useful to the doer than to him for whom it is done.* On another stela the thought is expanded: *It means nothing out of your coffers, nor is it irksome to the mouth of him who says it.*[46] What bathos that a people who had staked their hopes upon the luxury of their tombs should have to plead thus, whining like beggars that it will cost the passer-by nothing and may well bring him luck!

I have been able to indicate the nature of Egyptian funerary preparations only in the barest outlines, and have said nothing about the heart-scarabs, the ushebti-figures, the Canopic jars, and all the other appurtenances which were ingeniously devised for the protection of the dead. These material arrangements found their spiritual counterpart in a plethora of theories as to a man's fate in the hereafter.[47] One common view was that the soul was translated to the sky to follow in the train of the sun-bark, while in another view the deceased went in and out of the tomb pursuing his earthly avocations. The soul might also assume various shapes or be identified with some powerful deity. Most prevalent of all was the affirmation that the dead man became identified with the great god Osiris himself. Let it not be imagined that these discrepant theories were the opinions of different sects or of individuals in different grades of education. Although in a complex civilization like that of Ancient Egypt one must always reckon with divergent strata of belief, there is ample evidence to show that the most varying conceptions were held at the same time, and were indeed often asserted in one and the same breath. To quote but one rather lengthy example from the Eighteenth Dynasty:[48]

Thou shalt come in and go out, thy heart rejoicing, in the favour of the Lord of the Gods, a good burial (being thine) after a venerable old age, when age has come, thou assuming thy place in the coffin, and joining earth in the high ground of the West. (Thou shalt) change into a living soul, and surely he will have power to obtain bread and water and air; and thou shalt take shape as a heron or swallow, as a falcon or a bittern, whichever thou pleasest. Thou shalt cross in the ferry-boat and shalt not turn back. Thou shalt sail on the waters of the flood, and thy life shall start afresh. Thy soul shall not depart from thy corpse, and thy soul shall become divine with the blessed dead. The perfect souls shall speak to thee, and thou shalt be an equal amongst them in receiving what is given upon earth. Thou shalt have power over water, shalt inhale air, and shalt be surfeited with the desires of thy heart. Thine eyes shall be given thee so as to see, and thine ears so as to hear, thy mouth speaking and thy feet walking. Thy arms and thy shoulders shall move for thee, thy flesh shall be firm, thy muscles shall be easy, and thou shalt exult in all thy limbs. Thou shalt examine thy body (and find it) whole and sound, no ill whatsoever adhering to thee. Thine own true heart shall be with thee, yea thou shalt have thy former heart. Thou shalt go up to the sky, and shalt penetrate the netherworld in all forms that thou likest.

Was the prince Paḥeri thus addressed to remain confined to the sepulchral chamber with his soul, or was he to wander the earth wherever he pleased? Was he to ascend to Heaven or to descend into Hell? Was he to keep his human form or to become a heron or a hawk? All these possibilities are promised to him, and can hardly be reconciled on the assumption that the writer of the passage meant them to be consecutive. The kaleidoscopic variety of the future so depicted doubtless added to its impressiveness in the writer's eyes, and the very inconsistency of the conceptions thus combined will have conferred upon them a mystic power. But looking behind all this make-

believe we discern clearly enough a radical scepticism as to man's fate in the hereafter. The emotions
conjured up a brightly coloured picture, but the
reason, had it been consulted, would have told
another tale. Nevertheless the conservatism of
the Egyptians made them persevere in elaborate
funerary preparations to the very end of Pharaonic
history, despite their inevitable knowledge of that
spoliation of the tombs which everywhere met
the eye.

Only the more thoughtful discerned the truth,
and these reacted in different ways. We have
several copies of a harper's song describing the
transitoriness of human life, deploring the de-
struction of the tombs, and drawing the con-
clusion that it is best to eat, drink and be merry,
for tomorrow we must die and pass to a land
whence there is no return.[49] A Twentieth Dynasty effusion which has only recently come to
light and certainly borrowed from the afore-
mentioned song adopts another standpoint:
tombs perish, and children forget you; it is much
better to write books; your writings will keep
your memory alive.[50] A very curious Middle

Kingdom papyrus appears to recommend suicide as the only remedy, and in a passage of considerable beauty death is praised as a happy event.[51] But there also existed a view of the tomb as a place of rest and tranquillity. A poem expressing this thought is inscribed on a tomb-wall exactly opposite the song of our hedonistic harper, and is so brave an answer to that early precursor of Epicurus that I will quote it *in extenso*:

I have heard those songs that are in the ancient tombs, and what they tell extolling life on earth and belittling the region of the dead. Wherefore do they thus concerning the land of eternity, the just and fair, which has no terrors? Wrangling is its abhorrence, and no man there girds himself against his fellow. It is a land against which none can rebel; all our kinsfolk rest within it since the earliest day of time. The offspring of millions of millions are come thither, every one. For none may tarry in the land of Egypt, none there is who has not passed yonder. The span of earthly things is as a dream; but a fair welcome is given to him who has reached the West.[52]

Let us now sum up our results. That the Egyptians felt no great fear of their dead can be affirmed on many grounds, of which perhaps the most important is the extreme prevalence of tomb-robbery. Disease and misfortune were indeed sometimes attributed to the dead, but magic was an efficacious remedy in such instances, and dead parents also could usually be called upon to counter evil influences from this source. At all events a fear of the dead played no part in the development of Egyptian funerary observances, which were, on the contrary, due partly to the fear of annihilation and partly to the knowledge that but little care of the dead could be expected from the living. Accordingly every man who possessed the means prepared his tomb and funerary equipment during his own lifetime, entering into contracts for the upkeep of the food-offerings with soul-priests especially appointed for that very purpose. All this availed him little, however, since such contracts rapidly fell into abeyance, while the treasures buried with the dead proved an irresistible temptation to tomb-robbers. I will end with some moralizing which I trust will not be felt to be priggish. The Egyptians present the tragic spectacle of a people with exaggerated demands for their own persons, but without a corresponding sense of obligation towards others. There is something truly pathetic about all the care they lavished on their burials in face of the certainty that these would soon fall a prey to the plunderer. If they had possessed a proper sense of reverence, they would have tended the cult of their ancestors as jealously as the Chinese, from whatever motive, always did. With such an outlook perhaps they would not have reaped the eternal felicity for which they hoped, but at least they would have saved themselves from that sense of futile effort which may be read between the lines of almost every funerary inscription.

NOTES

The standpoints adopted in this lecture are approximately the same as those expressed by me in previous writings: in the article *Life and Death (Egyptian)* contributed to Hastings' *Encyclopaedia of Religion and Ethics*; also in the concluding chapter of my text in Davies and Gardiner, *The Tomb of Amenemhēt* (Theban Tombs Series, vol. I), 1915. Other scholars' estimates are not, so far as I can see, wholly in accord. In my opinion they mostly fail to emphasize the plain inference to be drawn from the wide prevalence of tomb-robbery, and do not recognize the fundamental scepticism which is evidenced by the plethora of theories and practical devices invented by the Egyptians with a view to their happiness in the hereafter. It must, however, be freely admitted that the problems here discussed involve a rather exceptional degree of subjective appreciation.

My lecture being primarily addressed to anthropologists and other non-Egyptological students, references have been given to a number of recent books and articles where the various topics touched upon are discussed at greater length.

1. H. Kees, *Totenglauben und Jenseitsvorstellungen der alten Ägypter*, 1926, pp. 2 foll.

2. J. H. Breasted, *The Dawn of Conscience*, 1933, p. 45. Kees (*op. cit.* p. 38) also stresses the frequency with which skeletons and bones were seen, but uses the fact only to explain the introduction of mummification.

3. In full: "O ye who live and exist, who love life and hate death, whosoever shall pass by this tomb; as ye love life and hate death, so shall ye offer to me with what is in your hands. If nought is in your hands, ye shall speak (thus) with your mouths: a thousand of bread and beer, of oxen and geese, of alabaster vessels and of linen, a thousand of all pure things to the revered Enyotef, son of Enyotef, son of Khuu", Cairo 20003, *a*, 1–5. So too often elsewhere, e.g. Cairo 20030, *i*, 2–6; 20515, *b*, 3–5; 20530, *b*, 1–6; Louvre C 177, 2 foll.; Brit. Mus. 1059.

4. Sir J. G. Frazer, *The Fear of the Dead in Primitive Religion*, vol. I, 1933; vol. II, 1934.

5. So rightly H. R. Hall, *Ancestor-worship and cult of the dead* (*Egyptian*), in Hastings' *Encyclopaedia of Religion and Ethics*.

6. See A. Moret, *Le rituel du culte divin journalier en Égypte*, in *Annales du Musée Guimet*, 1902.

7. This would follow, of course, from the mere archaeological discoveries, even if we had no documentary evidence, since the dead cannot bury themselves.

8. I can discover no justification for Breasted's assertion, *op. cit.* pp. 117–18: "Over and over again we find that the massive tombs of the pyramid cemeteries were erected by the son for the departed father, and that a splendid interment was arranged by the son." The evidence quoted by him in his earlier work, *Development of Religion and Thought in Ancient Egypt*, p. 64, n. 1, proves only that some additions were made by the son, and it has rightly been the accepted view that nobles, like the

Pharaoh himself, prepared their own tombs and burial equipment during their own lifetimes. A typical specimen of the kind of evidence on which Breasted relies (K. Sethe, *Urkunden*, I, 8, 14–17) may be translated as follows: "It was his eldest son, the overseer of *ka*-priests and scribe Ptaḥiutni, who made this for him after he had been buried in the goodly West, according as he had told him about it when he was alive upon his feet." (From the jambs of the outer door of a maṣṭaba.) It is not clear to what "made this" refers. Does it mean merely the door? If it is a claim to have constructed the entire tomb, it is a false claim, as the words "after he had been buried" clearly show. For the latter phrase in other similar cases, see Sethe, *op. cit.* I, 9, 5; 15, 17; 33, 9; 227, 12. 16; 228, 17.

9. The paragraphs with which Prof. Erman begins his chapter on "Totenglaube" (*Die Religion der Ägypter*, 1934, p. 207) seem to me open to very serious objections. He writes: "Wenn es eine Seite gibt, in der sich das ägyptische Volk von anderen unterscheidet, so ist es die Fürsorge, die es seinen Toten zuwendet. Während die Hebräer oder die Griechen nicht viel und nicht gern von dem Schicksal ihrer Abgeschiedenen sprechen, denkt der Ägypter unablässig an sie; er bemüht sich, sie zu pflegen und für ihr Ergehen zu sorgen, und möchte auch die Erinnerung an sie nicht untergehen lassen. Anfangs hat diese Totenpflege gewiss keinen anderen Grund gehabt als den natürlichen allgemein menschlichen, die Liebe zu den Angehörigen." It is true, as indeed I have asserted on

p. 8, that according to the Egyptians' own professions filial piety lay at the base of all their funerary observances. It is even possible that in prehistoric times this sentiment really impelled them to fill their parents' tombs with the chattels and weapons they had prized during their lives, though it would agree better with what Sir James Frazer has found in other lands if we postulated a fear of the dead as the real motive force. Concerning those remote ages it is impossible to dogmatize for lack of written evidence. Erman realizes that filial piety no longer suffices to explain the elaborate preparations for the hereafter made by the Egyptians of the Old Kingdom and later; and he gives a curious explanation of these: "Solchen Anstrengungen würde sich das ägyptische Volk nicht während dreier Jahrtausende unterzogen haben, wenn sich nicht jenem ursprünglichen Motive der Pietät allmählich noch andere Beweggründe beigesellt hätten. Es waren das die Vorstellungen über das Jenseits und über das Weiterleben der Toten...." But surely these beliefs, like the material funerary preparations which reflect them, were the outcome of the Egyptians' intense anxiety as to their own future fate; they were, in fact, results or symptoms, rather than causes. The fundamental error lies in not recognizing that the whole body of funerary doctrine and practice, in its developed form, arose from the Egyptians' preoccupation *with themselves*, not from their disinterested solicitude for, or love of, the other-dead.

10. See above p. 27, and below n. 43.

11. (Sir) E. A. W. Budge, *Book of the Dead*, 1898, Text, 113, 7–8; 293, 12; 365, 11–366, 1; 389, 13–14; 477, 6; without "men", *op. cit.* 298, 12–13; 308, 15; P. Lacau, *Textes religieux*, 16, 13. In all these passages the dead are indicated in two terms, namely *ȝḫw* and *m(w)tw*, of which the former, perhaps best rendered as "the blessed dead", may refer to dead men of rank only, while the latter, simply the participle from the verb "to die", would mean the rank and file of the dead.

12. See Davies and Gardiner, *op. cit.* p. 19, n. 1.

13. See Erman and Grapow, *Wörterbuch der ägyptischen Sprache*, vol. iii, p. 2, under C ii.

14. 1, 51.

15. J. E. Quibell, *Excavations at Saqqara* (1912–1914), Pl. xxxi, with p. 13.

16. Particularly in the Turin Canon of Kings, see E. Meyer, *Ägyptische Chronologie*, p. 118.

17. Pleyte and Rossi, *Papyrus de Turin*, Pl. 135, l. 10. Still more emphatically A. H. Gardiner, *Hieratic Papyri in the British Museum* (Chester Beatty Gift), 1935, p. 73: "Should Osiris not know his name, I will not allow him (i.e. Osiris) to fare down to Busiris, I will not allow him to sail up to Abydos, I will tear out his soul and annihilate his corpse, and I will set fire to every tomb of his." In reference to the last clause, note that various towns laid claim to the possession of some member of the body of Osiris, so that he possessed many tombs.

18. See Erman and Grapow, *op. cit.* vol. v, p. 303, top. Also K. Sethe, *Urkunden*, iv, 6, 14, and often.

19. This thought finds expression in various ways, for example in the euphemistic word *ḫp(y)t* for "death", literally "departure", and in the phrase *zbi(?) n kȝ-f* "gone to his *ka* (soul)", i.e. dead. Also in the image of the "ferryman", an Egyptian Charon, see Erman, *op. cit.* p. 217. The idea of death as a transition is implied very clearly in the use of the term "yonder", literally "there", for the world of the dead; *ntyw im* "those who are yonder" was a common euphemism for "the dead".

20. See H. Grapow in *Zeitschrift für ägyptische Sprache*, vol. XLVII, pp. 100 foll.

21. Budge, *op. cit.* p. xxiv, heading to Chapter XLV.

22. *Ibid.*, heading to Chapter XLIII.

23. *Op. cit.* p. xxiii, heading to Chapter XXX A.

24. *Op. cit.* p. xxiv, heading to Chapter XLIV; p. xxxvi, heading to Chapter CLXXVI. Compare too the "Spell for not perishing, but remaining living in the necropolis", *op. cit.* p. xxiv, heading to Chapter XLVI.

25. A. Erman, *Zaubersprüche für Mutter und Kind*, p. 11 (1, 9), in *Abhandlungen der kön. Preuss. Akademie der Wissenschaften*, 1901.

26. In characterizing the Egyptians as intensely individualistic, I must guard myself against misunderstandings. By individualistic I here mean prone to self-aggrandizement, an Egyptian tendency of which the Great Pyramid supplies the most eloquent proof. There is perhaps no other people which has carried to such lengths boasting concerning their virtues and achievements; the inscrip-

tions are full of it. I am not here considering the other senses in which the Egyptians may be judged to be among the least individualistic of mankind, e.g. in the uniformity and anonymity of their art and literature. This and the cognate questions have been interestingly discussed of late; see A. de Buck, *Het typische en het individueele bij de Egyptenaren*, Leyden, 1929; W. Wolf, *Individuum und Gemeinschaft in der ägyptischen Kultur*, Glückstadt, 1935.

27. διόπερ παρὰ Χαλδαίοις, παρ' οἷς διακέκριται καθαρὸς ὁ πρὸς μόνους τοὺς θεοὺς λόγος, οὐδαμοῦ ἀπειλὴ λέγεται· Αἰγύπτιοι δὲ συμμιγνύοντες ἅμα μετὰ τῶν θειῶν συνθημάτων καὶ τοὺς δαιμονίους λόγους, χρῶνται ἔστιν ὅτε καὶ ταῖς ἀπειλαῖς. G. Parthey, *Iamblichi de Mysteriis liber*, 1857, p. 249.

28. H. Sottas, *La préservation de la propriété funéraire dans l'ancienne Égypte*, 1913. I would recommend the Introduction to this book as agreeing closely with my own estimate of the facts.

29. See T. E. Peet, *The Great Tomb-robberies of the Twentieth Dynasty*, 1930.

30. Some writers have sought to minimize this sacrilegious trait in the Egyptian character by ascribing the tomb-robberies to periods of political unrest. Certainly there will have been a great increase of that crime at such periods, see various passages in the papyrus published by me in *The Admonitions of an Egyptian Sage*, Leipzig, 1909, e.g. 7, 8: "Behold, the possessors of tombs are destroyed upon the high desert. He who could not make for himself a coffin is (now lord of a) Treasury."

31. See my article *Magic (Egyptian)* in Hastings' *Encyclopaedia of Religion and Ethics*, § 7.

32. See two passages quoted *loc. cit.*

33. An elaborate list of ways in which a man could meet his death is given in a magical papyrus in the Turin Museum, Pleyte and Rossi, *op. cit.* Pl. 120, 8–121, 11; fragment of a similar list, (Sir) W. M. F. Petrie, *Gizeh and Rifeh*, 1907, Pl. xxvii O, with p. 27.

34. For references see p. 11 in the book referred to in n. 36.

35. The original teems with awkward constructions and difficult phrases. For a more literal translation, with philological remarks, see the book named in the next note.

36. A. H. Gardiner and K. Sethe, *Egyptian Letters to the Dead*, 1928.

37. One now in the Chicago Museum, *Journal of Egyptian Archaeology*, vol. xvi, p. 19; another in the Louvre, *op. cit.* vol. xx, p. 157.

38. That Egyptian funerary observances were not based upon a fear of the dead (except possibly in prehistoric times where the fact is unverifiable, see above n. 9) is emphatically stated by Erman, *op. cit.* p. 245, footnote: "Der Gedanke, dass man den Toten aus Furcht vor ihnen 'geopfert' habe, um sie so zu besänftigen, ist ganz unägyptisch."

39. For the best general account see G. Elliot Smith and W. R. Dawson, *Egyptian Mummies*, 1924. See too K. Sethe, *Zur Geschichte der Einbalsamierung bei den*

Ägyptern und einiger damit verbundener Bräuche, in *Sitzungsb. d. Preuss. Akad. d. Wissensch.*, Phil.-Hist. Klasse, 1934, XIII.

40. See P. Lacau, *Suppressions et modifications de signes dans les textes funéraires*, in *Zeitschrift für ägyptische Sprache*, vol. LI, pp. 1 foll.

41. For a good summary description of the tombs of noblemen of the Fourth Dynasty see G. A. Reisner, *The Servants of the Ka*, in *Bulletin of the Museum of Fine Arts* (Boston), vol. XXXII, 1934, pp. 1–12; in much greater detail, H. Junker, *Gîza I*, 1929; *Gîza II*, 1934, in *Denkschriften d. Akad. d. Wissensch. in Wien*. The decorations and meaning of a Theban tomb of the Eighteenth Dynasty are discussed in detail in Davies and Gardiner, *The Tomb of Amenemḥēt*, 1915. In the present very general statement no attempt has been made to distinguish the standpoints of different periods, the sole object having been to characterize the Egyptian attitude from a very broad point of view.

42. See A. M. Blackman, *The Ka-house and the Serdab*, in *Journal of Egyptian Archaeology*, vol. III, pp. 250–4; also A. H. Gardiner, *A New Masterpiece of Egyptian Sculpture*, in *op. cit.* vol. IV, pp. 1–3. The use of statues in tombs is thought to be a Lower Egyptian innovation by H. Ranke, *The Origin of the Egyptian Tomb Statue*, in *The Harvard Theological Review*, vol. XXVIII, 1935, pp. 45 foll.

43. For the number and functions of the *ka*-priests see the article of G. A. Reisner quoted in n. 41 above. An elaborate study of the most extensive contract of the kind

(Twelfth Dynasty) is given by the same author in his article *The tomb of Hepzefa, Nomarch of Siût*, in *Journal of Egyptian Archaeology*, vol. v, pp. 79–98; see too F. Ll. Griffith, *Tomb-endowment in Ancient Egypt*, in *Zeitschrift für ägyptische Sprache*, vol. LX, pp. 83–4. The large amount of food which a local temple might distribute, after use as divine offerings, to the *ka*-servants of nobles having doubtless made contracts with the priests, is well seen in the papyrus of accounts published by L. Borchardt, *Besoldungsverhältnisse von Priestern im mittleren Reich*, in *op. cit.* vol. XL, pp. 113–17. The texts of the few known Old Kingdom contracts are all published by K. Sethe in his *Urkunden des alten Reiches*, but a sound philological study of them is still outstanding.

44. Stelae of the Middle Kingdom mostly depict or describe the eldest son as "making to live the name" (*sꜥnḫ rn*) of his father. The phrase appears to refer only to the dedication of the stela, which may indeed in many or most cases have been effected by the son.

45. See above the specimen quoted in n. 3.

46. Such phrases have been collected by W. Spiegelberg, *Eine Formel der Grabsteine*, in *Zeitschrift für ägyptische Sprache*, vol. XLV, pp. 67–71.

47. See Erman, *op. cit.* ch. XIV, *Der Totenglaube*, and Kees, *op. cit.*; in the latter book a laudable, but perhaps sometimes over-daring, attempt is made to trace the development of such beliefs at different periods.

48. K. Sethe, *Urkunden*, IV (second edition, 1930), pp. 113–15.

49. An English translation in A. Erman, *The Literature of the Ancient Egyptians*, translated by A. M. Blackman, 1927, p. 133.

50. A. H. Gardiner, *Hieratic Papyri in the British Museum* (Chester Beatty Gift), 1935, pp. 38–9.

51. Translated A. Erman, *op. cit.* pp. 86–92.

52. A. H. Gardiner, *In praise of Death*, in *Proceedings of the Society of Biblical Archaeology*, vol. xxxv, pp. 165–9.

www.ingramcontent.com/pod-product-compliance
Ingram Content Group UK Ltd.
Pitfield, Milton Keynes, MK11 3LW, UK
UKHW042141280225
455719UK00001B/13

9 781107 689268